This Book Is Presented To

_____

By _____

On The Date Of

_____

A NOTE FROM THE AUTHOR

Probably any youth minister or person who works with young people could have written this book better than me. Therefore, I'm thankful for those who plan the Youth Workers arm of the **Freed-Hardeman University** Lectures for the invitation to speak at the luncheon, which promoted me to put this together.

Also, I'd like to pay an homage or nod to **Heritage Christian University**, who asked me to speak at their inaugural chapel for 2009; as well as **21st Century Christian**, who picked that up and put it in "A Minister's Heart."

Special thanks to the one and only **Bradley Gean** whose masterful artistry and design give greater meaning and impact to our little words in this little work.

I dedicate this book to my two sons (who know what that smell is), their wives who also serve in youth ministry, and to the many youth ministers who have impacted their lives, impact my life, and who excite the spiritual minds of our most valuable asset: our children.

These folks are either our greatest danger or blessing-- but more often than not, the ones I have known have been the later and for that I praise God.

Dale Jenkins

(dale@edge.net)

To read more of Dale's writings go to
www.TheJenkinsInstitute.com.

Be sure to catch "The Blog That Binds", "Thoughts from the Mound", and "Hope & Expectation" (the bi-monthly online magazine produced by Dale and his brother, Jeff.)

Dale can also be heard on
www.TheEquipNetwork.com
through various podcast there including iPreach and MinistryGeek.

I WANT TO TELL YOU ABOUT "YOUR MINISTRY"...

You're going to pour your heart into a youth work to see it suffer because two eighth grade girls can't get along over a boy.

There's going to be considerable discussion over what to call you—
"youth worker", "youth minister", "minister to youth", "associate minister",
or "family minister" –
when you just want to be called "Trae."

YOUTH MINISTER/ SONG LEADER

Youth Minister/ Educational Director

Youth Minister/ Involvement Minister

Youth Minister/ Yard Boy

A church is going to want you to be a "Youth Minister Slash..."

These people don't know what youth ministry really is.

You are going to stay up at
ungodly hours playing games to
connect with kids so you can
get into their hearts...
only to be condemned
by an elder, who can't
understand why you don't make
it into the office by 6 A.M. like
he had to.

You're going to wonder

WHAT

that SMELL is.

You are going to take less than half the pay of the "pulpit minister" (a term you wonder what it means), to be told you have to wash the church van once a month... so the older people can use it.

You are going to miss many of the "big church" events...

...because somebody has to "do something" with the kids.

You are going to teach on
Sundays...

Wednesdays...

Vacation Bible School...

and at every other
event possible.

Your job is going to involve
**video games, music,
and hanging out with
young people...**

Cool…

Some **preacher** is going
to THINK your job is
video games, music,
and hanging out with
young people...

...NOT
COOL.

You are going to be
expected to be
an expert on
"youth culture"-

whatever that is...

You are going to be asked to preach once a month because some folks think that as a paid minister you ought to have to "earn your pay."

Those same folks are going to rip your sermon to shreds and complain to the elders that they wished you preached like the regular guy.

You are going to sacrifice
many evenings away from your
wife
and your own kids
to take "their kids" bowling...
to a youth rally... on a retreat...

Somebody is going
to get hurt.

You're going to wonder where the summer went.

Some young lady is going to accuse you of something inappropriate.

You will learn to guard your reputation.

You're going to wonder
WHAT THAT SMELL IS

... AGAIN.

When the budget gets cut,
yours will likely go
before the budget for:
mission work,
any other ministry,
the secretary, or even the
church janitor.

You are going to study hours
to present a lesson in Bible
class,
only to have it sabotaged by:
(Multiple choice here)

1) A girl who is so hot none of
the boys hear a word you say
2) A guy so cool none of the
girls hear a word you say
3) A cat fight
4) An announcement
the elders made
5) Something that happened
at school that day

Someone in your youth group is going to die.

The built-up emotion is going to rip your heart out.

A jealous preacher is going to call you a danger to the church... when what he really means is he thinks you are more popular than he is and his ego (or his wife) can't handle it.

Your wife is going to develop an ability to be frank –

Learn to laugh with her often.

You are going to be tested by mean and little people...

Pray for them.

They are going to tempt you again...

Talk to them.

You are going to learn that some of them are just little people who have no real interest in right.

Picture them with a big clown nose and big floppy shoes.

You'll learn then to just smile when you see them coming.

You are going to be temped to laugh at others.

Learn to laugh more at yourself... except for that clown-nosed person.

You're going to change the life of a child with your teaching on grace, forgiveness, & commitment.

A father is going to be mad at you because his son is more interested in Bible study than throwing a baseball.

You're going to feel like Christ... Don't forget what they did to Him.

A stink bomb is
in your future.

You are going to be interrogated by a helicopter parent, asking more questions than a terrorism task force, **all to let their little baby girl go ice skating.**

You are going to get tired of it and invite that parent to go along with you...

You are going to regret that invitation.

You are going to be "allowed" to live in the old "preacher's house..."
(Accommodations none of the elders wives would ever stand for with their own families!)

You better be thankful and never mention that:

- THE CEILING IS SAGGING,
- ONLY ONE ELEMENT IN THE HOT WATER HEATER IS WORKING,
- THAT THERE'S A HOLE IN THE FOUNDATION THAT ALLOWS SMALL ANIMALS TO COME AND GO AT WILL,
- THE ELECTRICAL SYSTEM LOOKS LIKE SOMETHING THAT MACGYVER WIRED ON A THREE-DAY-DRUNK,
- (OR THAT) THE ROOF LEAKS.

And, oh yeah, several people will have keys to your house and periodically and unexpectedly use them!
You're going to make the mistake of telling the youth group to make themselves at home, and they will... every day!

You are going to be human.

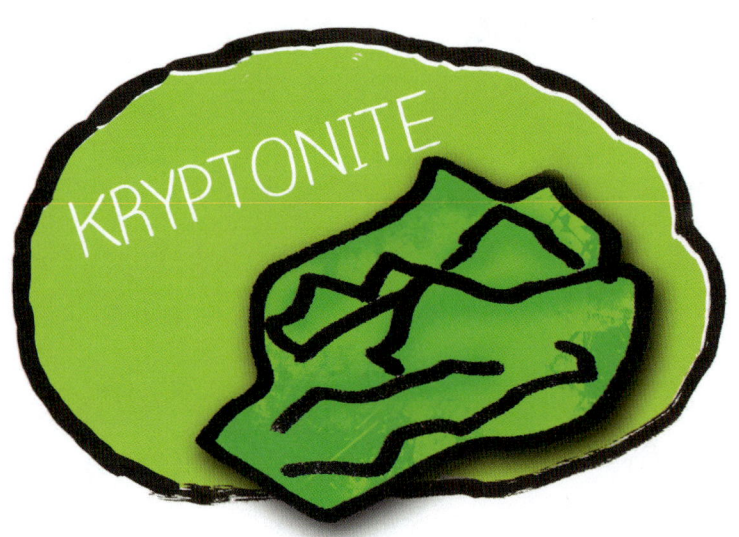

KRYPTONITE

You are going to be accused of being in the office "**too much**"... You are going to be accused of being in the office "**too little.**"

You're going to resist having Facebook only to learn that it is **the best method to communicate** with your young people...

Then you are going to be accused of being on FB too much (during those "rare occasions" you are at the office.)

One way or another –
You are going to track down
that smell!

You're going to be told you are
trying to be too
"cool" by leaders, who at some
point will fire you
because you "no longer
connect" with the kids.

You will take a teen to an event
at a Christian college...
They will have the time of their life
and want to go school there.

Then, their mom is going to be
upset because her "future
Michael Jordan" no longer wants
to go to a school where
they might be spotted to play
pro ball.
You saw him play...

You know you did the right thing.

Your son will be called the youth program mascot.

You will laugh... and then think... REALLY?

34. THOU SHALT HAVE SERVICE PROJECTS TWICE A MONTH, ON WEDNESDAYS. 35. WHEN THE KIDS CAN'T: YOU STILL CAN-ETH, TIMOTHY.

You are going to
be told that the young people
need to rake leaves for the
older people –
you're going to
wonder where that is in the
Bible... It is... I'm sure it is…
It must be.

You will be asked deeper
theological questions than
you are prepared to answer.

First Corinthians 10:3

Your faith will be tested... Your patience will be tested... Your energy will be tested..."You will remember that you cannot be tested beyond what you can endure.

You are going to take your infant daughter to work with you and an elder or a secretary will object.

You only did it so your wife could work and you could stay off food stamps.

You are going to be asked to
speak at "that event"
that you measure the success
of your ministry through.

You're going to come up with a perfect, heart pricking devotional... **but none of the kids will be there because there is an AAU tournament that weekend.**

You're going to be told sandals are not appropriate attire if you are serving at the head of the Lord's Table. You are going to reply that Jesus wore sandals... and you are going to be correct.

Buy a pair of big boy shoes, anyway. You'll lose that argument.

One of the kids in the youth group is going to do something really stupid...
and you are going to be held responsible for it.

(It will probably be an elder's kids. Just accept it.)

You're going to take the youth group on a positively life changing retreat –

A charge on the church credit cardis going to be questioned.

You're going to have to be better than the FBI at tracking down signatures.

You're going to attend more soccer games... football games... basketball games... recitals... plays... tennis matches... (Who goes to tennis matches?)... baseball games... swim meets... and chess tournaments... **than any coach.**

You're going to wonder if you have outlived your own effectiveness – often.

You are going to shed enough tears to fill a camp swimming pool **when you baptize a young person, who would have never known the Lord except through your ministry.**

Your house will become a haven for a teenaged boy trying to avoid his abusive father.

Your wife is going to love you,
respect you, and fight for you.

You will have a minister
who will minister to you.

You are going to be thanked over and over again by a young single mom because you were "the strongest and most wonderful man" in her sons' lives **and she sees that influence every day.**

AUTHENTIC LIVING=
AUTHENTIC LOVE

You are going to be real –
you are going to love and
be loved.

Your living room will be known as a center of praise.

Thank you

That silly girl is going to develop a heart of compassion **that glows and illuminates the whole church** – she's going to thank you.

That boy voted "Most Likely to Become a Terrorist" is going to become a great spiritual leader, who delights in sharing God's Word and love with others.

He will call you about once every month or so-just to hear your voice and say, 'thank you'.

Some young romance that developed in the group is going to do mission work in a third world country.

Your sacrifice will make their dirt floor mean nothing to them – because they have seen that love lives in houses that money can't buy.

You will get a call at
2am from someone who is
hurting – **because you are
the only person in the
world who they feel loved by.**

That boy making the
smell is going to grow up
and want to be a
youth minister **because
of your patience
and influence.**

You are going to attend
a graduation where the class
Valedictorian is going to
tell about their hero...
You will weep uncontrollably
when the senior shocks
you by calling your name.

You will laugh till you cry... You will cry... You will be content.

FICATE OF BIRTH

TIFY THAT Austin Trae Smith

WAS BORTH TO Fred & Laura Smith

9:17 AM ON November 23, 2018

Someone is going to name their child after you.

You will get to
be a part of a band of brothers,
some of your fellow youth
ministers,
who understand...
Listen to each other and avoid
jealousy like the plague.

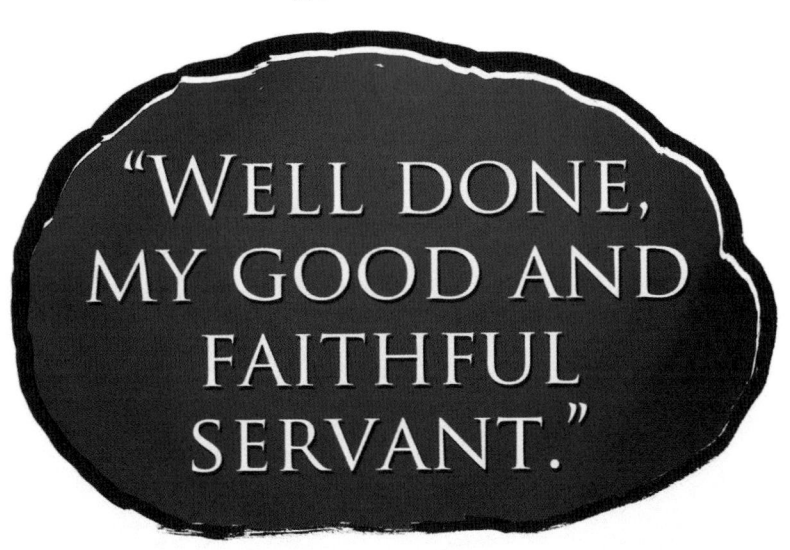

"WELL DONE, MY GOOD AND FAITHFUL SERVANT."

And people will be in heaven because you cared!

MAKE
SOMETHING
HAPPEN.

65814112R00046